KEEP THE CHANGE

Michele Heeney

KEEP
THE CHANGE

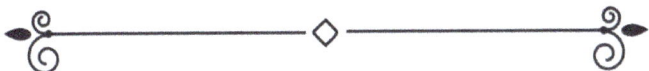

MICHELE HEENEY

ARPress
ILLUMINATING IDEAS,
EMPOWERING VOICES

ARPress
45 Dan Road Suite 5
Canton MA 02021
Hotline: 1(888) 821-0229
Fax: 1(508) 545-7580

Ordering Information:

Quantity sales. Special discounts are available on quantity purchases by corporations, associations, and others. For details, contact the publisher at the address above.

Printed in the United States of America.

ISBN-13:	Softcover	979-8-89356-343-6
	Hardcover	979-8-89356-345-0
	eBook	979-8-89356-344-3

Library of Congress Control Number: 2024906120

This is Michele Heeney's second book of poetry. Her first book was a collection of poems and color photographs. This book is mostly poems with a few of her black and white photos.

Michele has revised some of the older poems which appeared in her first book and she has written about twenty-five new poems for this book.

Some of the poems were written in Pennsylvania, where Michele grew up, some in California, where she lived for many years. Michele's new poems were all written in New Mexico where she currently lives.

This book represents a lifetime of poetry. Besides writing poetry, Michele managed a challenging career in the medical world and travels extensively.

Enjoy!

CONTENTS

Dedicated To Leonard Cohen,
My favorite poet.
Always.

THE POEMS

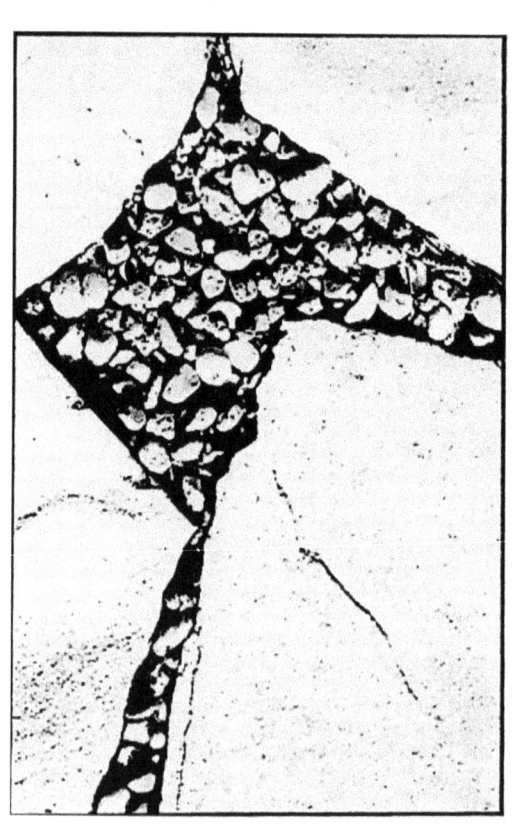

THE GOLDEN DOOR

The man
With a golden mind
Steps out of a
Great man's dream.
He is now
One of the chosen:
Keeper of the
Golden key.

Young man, be wise,
Lead us toward
Tranquil skies;
Sail us back
To the promised shore.
On our troubled
Ship of state,
Lead us through
The golden door.

NOTES FROM THE BORDERLANDS

Some of us are wildish;
We tear out all the pages.
Only roam the borders,
Hide the keys to all the cages.

We hear the angels chanting,
Know the devils' voices,
See the wounds in all the wounded,
Feel the grief of painful choices.

Some of us grow wild,
Grow in untamed ways,
Love with hearts wide open,
Sail uncharted days.

We run across scorched deserts,
Dance the highest ledge;
Be careful how you touch us,
We walk the sharpest edge.

Some of us are spirit,
We dwell in sacred places,
We are the shamans to the soul,
We own the scars seared on our faces.

DONE AT TWENTY-ONE

I've had twenty-one heartbreaks,
That's quite a few.
But I'll be double-dog-damned
If there'll be twenty-two.

There's been lots of blood,
Scar tissue and goo,
So I'm quite committed
To avoiding twenty-two.

CATCH ME

Please, catch me.
Don't let me win this game.
Use your biggest net,
Employ your fastest yacht.
Please, you really ought
To catch me.

Grab me by the hand,
Demand I understand
That I'm running out of time.
Lock me in your arms,
Catch me.

If I don't stop soon,
I'll run into the moon
Out in cold black space,
What a crazy race!
Please, catch me.

It appears the wind I seek;
It's not, I'm just too weak
To cease this silly game.
What I truly need
Is an end to all this speed.
Please, catch me.

If, while you're looking at the sky,
You see me flying by,
Kiss me on the mouth
And catch me.

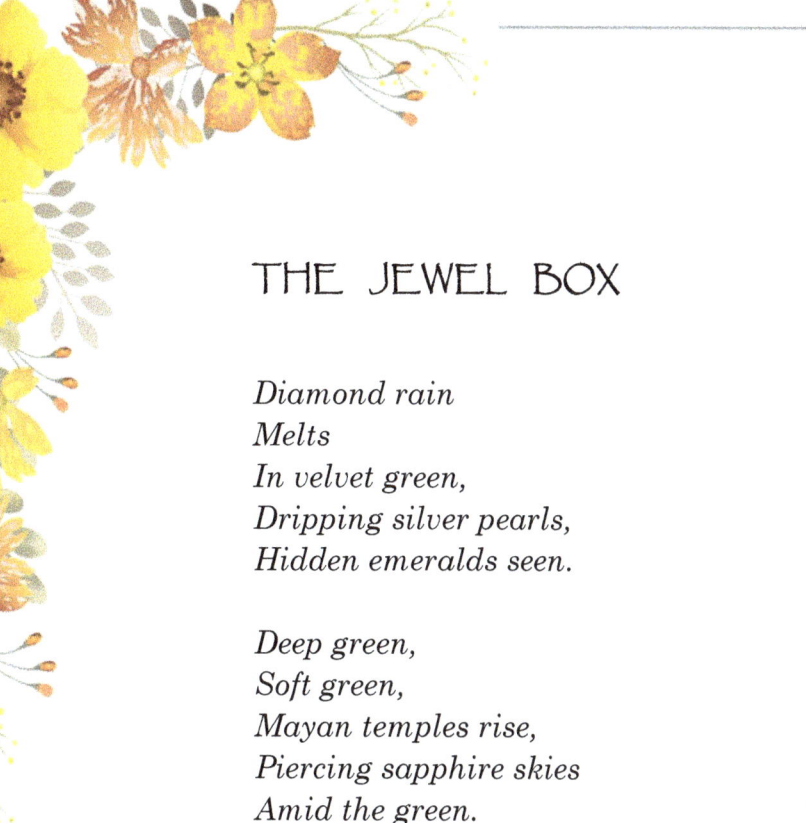

THE JEWEL BOX

Diamond rain
Melts
In velvet green,
Dripping silver pearls,
Hidden emeralds seen.

Deep green,
Soft green,
Mayan temples rise,
Piercing sapphire skies
Amid the green.

Dreamy,
Misty,
Luscious
Shades of green.

Tikal,
Painted all,
In vivid,
Brilliant
Stunning
Green.

MY DOOR

If you want
To be my boss,
Or if you want me
To be your mother,
Please, señor,
Save us both
Some pain,
Find yourself another lover.

But, if you seek
A partner equal,
Who will be
So true,
So sure,
Let me know
The day
The hour,
I'll be waiting
At my door.

SAD NOODLES

Sometimes life
Is so sad.

Take a long look
At sad,
Take a big drink
Of sad,
Sprinkle sad
On your noodles.

Eat,
Drink,
Then
    Spit
         It
           Out.

THE GLOBAL STORE

The store has lots of people here,
Some inside, some still out there.
I see a billion in the store,
Outside, about a billion more.

Tons of junk pushed round the place,
I think they'll soon run out of space.
Stacks of money flying in the air,
People buying like they just don't care.

I'm not quite sure just where I am,
Nothing looks like where I've been.
There are no doors, that much is clear.
Seems no one's getting out of here.

The store now calls me on the phone,
They can't seem to leave my phone alone.
They call me every single morning,
Even after of my lengthy warning.

There is no stopping all this now,
I've got to find a door somehow.
Just when I think I'm getting near,
The manager flashes a look of fear.

"Step back in line and spend some more,
Only the dead can leave the store."

FURRY WORRY MONKEY

That monkey's back again.

Jumps on my head,
Bangs into Buddha,
Jangles joy,
Pushes over peace,
Slices up silence.

I tell that monkey,
"We've plowed this field
One thousand times."

That monkey don't care,
Keeps on plowing.

Finally he's kaput.
Leaps off my head,
Jumps back out the window.

That crazy monkey!

THE MOST BEAUTIFUL BIRD IN THE WORLD

Could be you,
An ethereal spirit-bird;
One wing of wisdom,
One of compassion.

You could fly
On the winds of pure kindness
Into the golden corona
Of the sacred sun.

But you will need
Both wings.

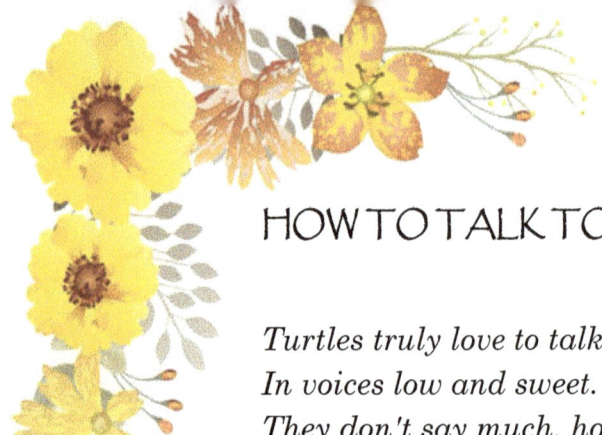

HOW TO TALK TO TURTLES

Turtles truly love to talk
In voices low and sweet.
They don't say much, however,
They're often quite discrete.

They've been around forever,
They know all kinds of things.
They can remember, for example,
When lizards had large wings.

The coolest thing by far
Is the house upon their backs.
They also walk around the place,
Rarely leaving any tracks.

They swim quite well to boot,
They swim both fast and deep.
On land they're hampered some,
On land, they mostly creep.

Now, the way to you talk to turtles is,
(As they are a cautious breed),
Slide up to them slowly,
They don't respond to speed.

Sit with them a week or two,
Then look them in the eye.
They sometimes seem so sad
It makes you want to cry.

But don't! Just hold their gaze
Then touch them without talking,
Perhaps a month or so,
Unless they take up walking.

If so, walk with them,
Maybe a year or more.
When they finally stop
Your legs may be quite sore.

Before you speak to turtles
Be certain that you think
Or inside their pretty shells
Their little heads will shrink.

Then, and only then, start a little chat.
Things will begin to flow;
You'll think, "It's great to talk to turtles."
This you will come to know.

Don't tell them lots of stupid stuff,
They're much too wise for this.
Keep the conversation meaningful,
End it with a kiss.

At last the time will come
When they know you're safe and kind,
They will listen sweetly
To whatever's on your mind.

If all this you'll remember
You'll have a friend forever.

MY BUTTERFLY NET

When I was young,
Young and free,
I ran all day
With the wind, with the birds
Through the trees.

Just breezing along
Catching whatever flew
Into my butterfly net.

Wow! The treasures I found!
Jewels of wonder and magic,
Incredible stuff,
Right out of the sky.

Now that God and I
Are secret lovers
I only aim to catch
His rare, elusive essence
The most incredible Stuff
Of All.

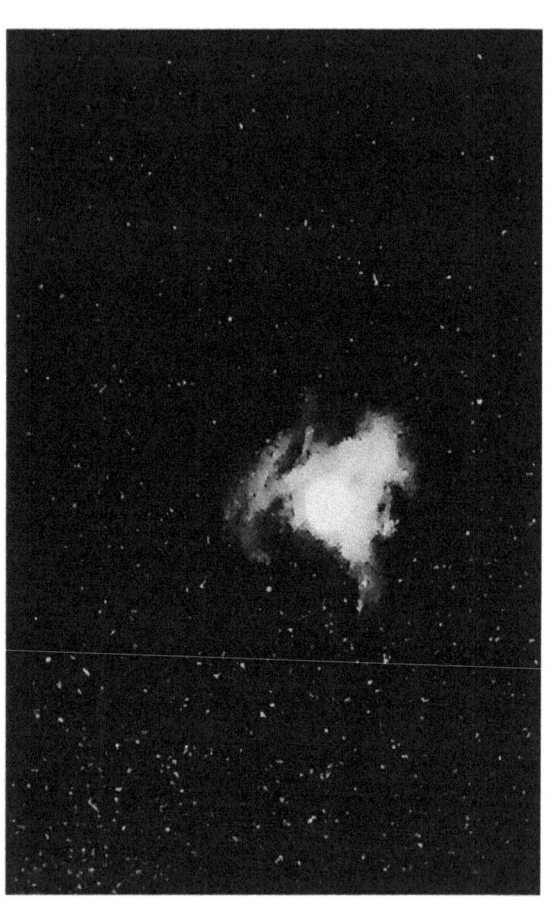

THE GREAT SPIRIT

Chasing after little loves
I am road weary and burning
In the driest desert.
Tripping over
Sharp cactus,
I stand with
Bloody legs,
A heart full
Of a gritty sort of silt.

When all the while
YOU were right here,
Succulent and sweet,
Lightly sitting on
My left breast.

PERCHANCE TO DREAM

Slowly slipping
Into the silent
Stream of sleep.
Sinking softly
Into quicksand
Half an acre deep.

Leaving sticky tangles
Far behind,
Toward the arms
Of vast, unconscious bliss.
Turning loose
The restless,
Racing mind

Traveling down
The edge
Of the indigo abyss.
Down, down,
Once again
To kiss
The constant lover
Sweet Morpheus.

MADRE DE LAS ESTRELLAS

Santa Maria,
Feminine Spirit of celestial lands,
Help me accept the abundant gifts
You have kindly placed in my hands.

Santa Maria,
Mother of the stars above,
Let me feel your deep blessings
Of gratitude and love.

Santa Maria,
May I be permitted
To forgive myself
For sins I have not committed.

Santa Maria,
Queen of time and space,
Hold me up to the moon
That I may kiss her snowy face.

A PINT OF GUINNESS, TOO

Someday I'll write a poem
As thick as Irish stew:
Big chunks of words so hearty,
Each sentence bold and true.

My poem: full of flavor
So rich, so full of juice,
Long simmered to perfection,
No compromise or truce.

Someday I'll write a poem
As fine as Irish stew.
When my poem's done just right
I'll bring a bowl to you.

DREAM SMOKE

Fuzzy
Foggy
Dreamt
Dream,
Vivid
Colored pieces
Briefly
Seen.

Fleeting
Fading
Faintly
Remembered
Notion,
Burning
Deeply
Felt emotion.

Hold it,
Keep it,
Catch the dream.

KITE FLYING

Yesterday
I tied a string
To my soul
A shining crimson kite.
Out to the autumn fields
To take it for a flight.

It scraped the clouds
So high, with ease
Flew with the wind
Near the yellow boughs
Of the cottonwood trees,
Soaring into space.

Today
I've searched the place.
Where is my kite?
Could it have flown
Too far, too high?
Lost in a jet stream
Into blue sky?

My loss is my sorrow;
Sadly I wait.
Perhaps tomorrow
My kite will turn up,
Caught on my garden gate.

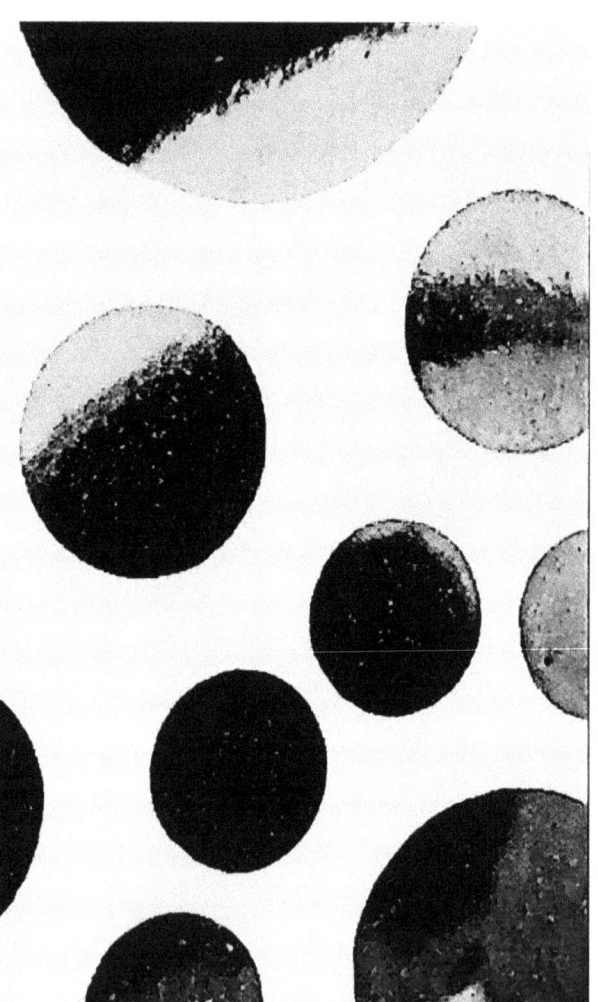

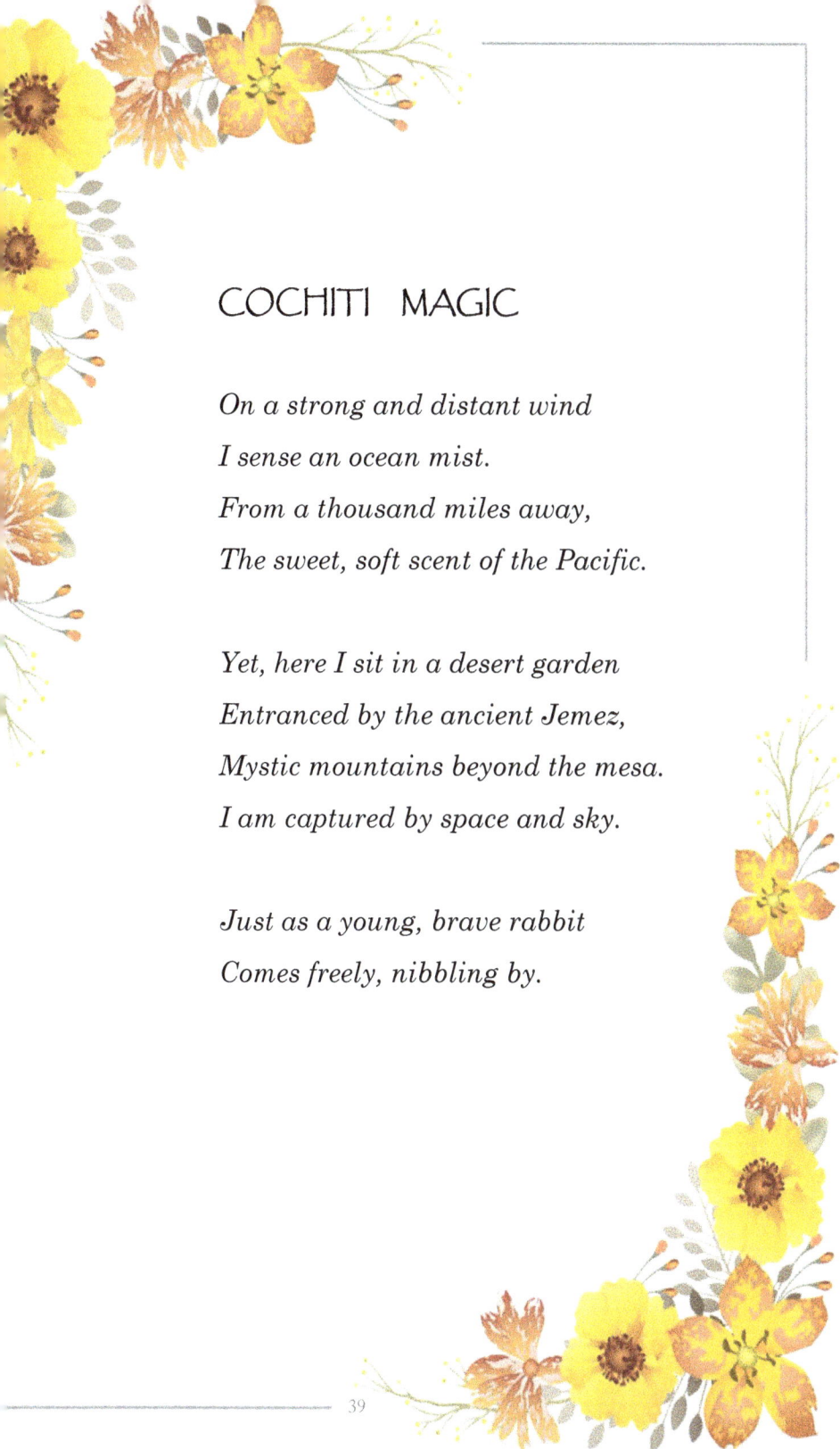

COCHITI MAGIC

On a strong and distant wind
I sense an ocean mist.
From a thousand miles away,
The sweet, soft scent of the Pacific.

Yet, here I sit in a desert garden
Entranced by the ancient Jemez,
Mystic mountains beyond the mesa.
I am captured by space and sky.

Just as a young, brave rabbit
Comes freely, nibbling by.

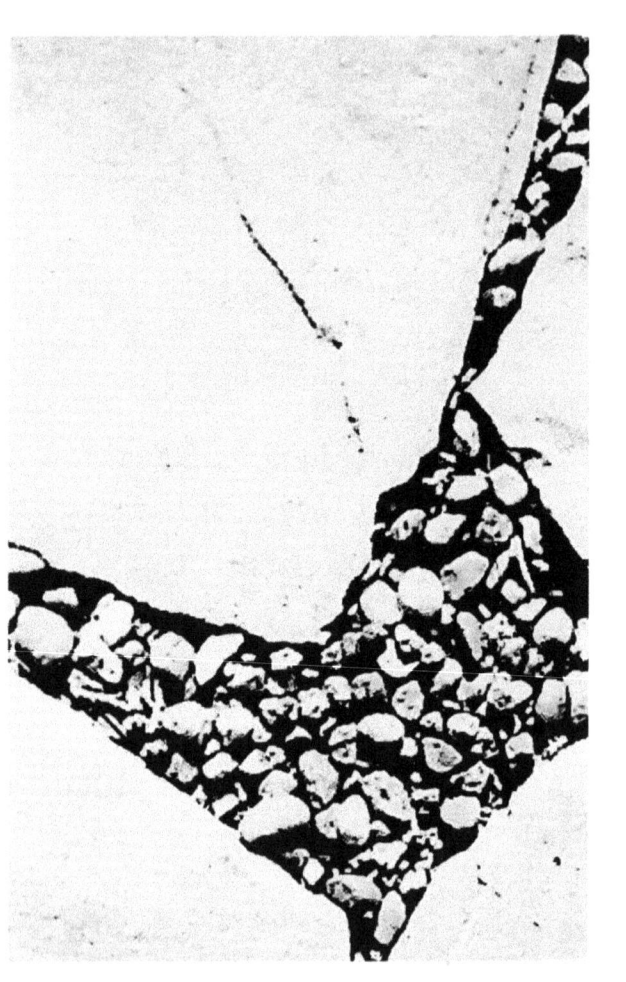

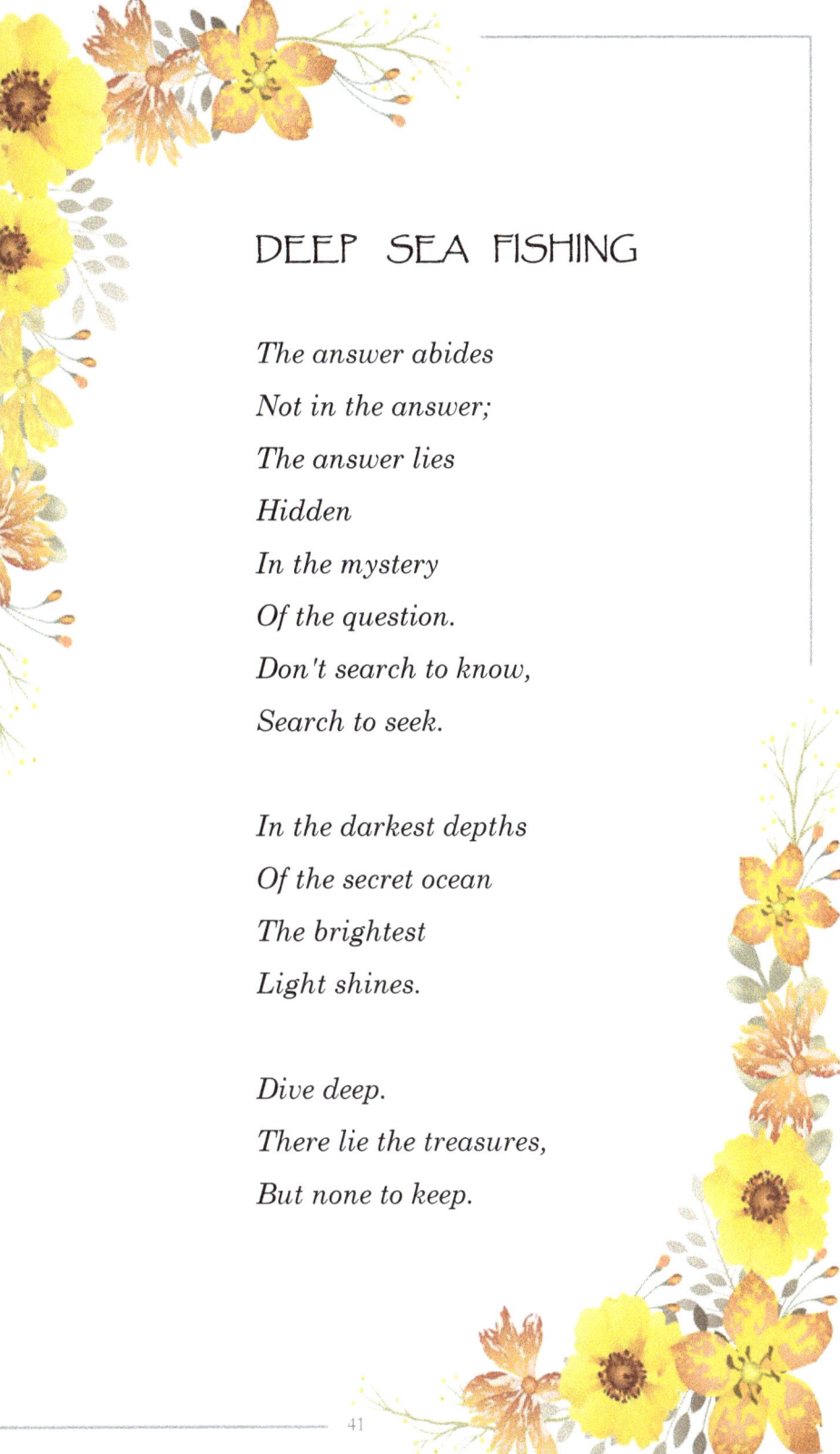

DEEP SEA FISHING

The answer abides
Not in the answer;
The answer lies
Hidden
In the mystery
Of the question.
Don't search to know,
Search to seek.

In the darkest depths
Of the secret ocean
The brightest
Light shines.

Dive deep.
There lie the treasures,
But none to keep.

KINGS OF PROGRESS

Earth melts
Weather rages
Oceans rise
The sun engages.

Your progress comes
At quite a cost:
Our world, our home
Soon may be lost.

Kings of change,
What have you done?

"You silly people,
Just move the sun!"

TO OLEG

Sitting beside my
Usual pile of words,
I sort through my mementos
Stashed in a dusty box
Within a secret room.

Here's the day we met:
The bright blue day
In Oaxaca,
We first felt
We had surely
Touched the sky.

Here, slow walks
By warm seas,
Crystal air
Of Big Sur hikes
Deep velvet nights.

But these are only words,
Colored shreds,
Old bones
Of what used to be.

And you –
A thousand miles
From me.

MY DOG HONEY

Honey went to heaven
In a bright blue boat,
Honey sailed away,
Didn't leave a note.

Can't quite believe it,
She'd up and leave it–
Honey went to heaven
In a boat.

Honey hit the road
In a new red car;
I never really thought
She'd ever get that far.

Honey took a powder
In a fast green truck,
Flying down the highway,
When the brakes got stuck.

Honey jumped a plane,
Gone for good I fear.
Honey flew to heaven
And left me here.

STANDING IN FRONT OF YOUR DOOR

I once had a blood red heart,
It sang,
Soared,
Sailed.

Now, it's stuck
To the sole
Of your shoe.

Now, there's a hole
In my chest
Where my heart
Used to be.

It's cold,
Sad,
Empty.

So, I'm here
At your doorstep
To say,
I want my heart back.

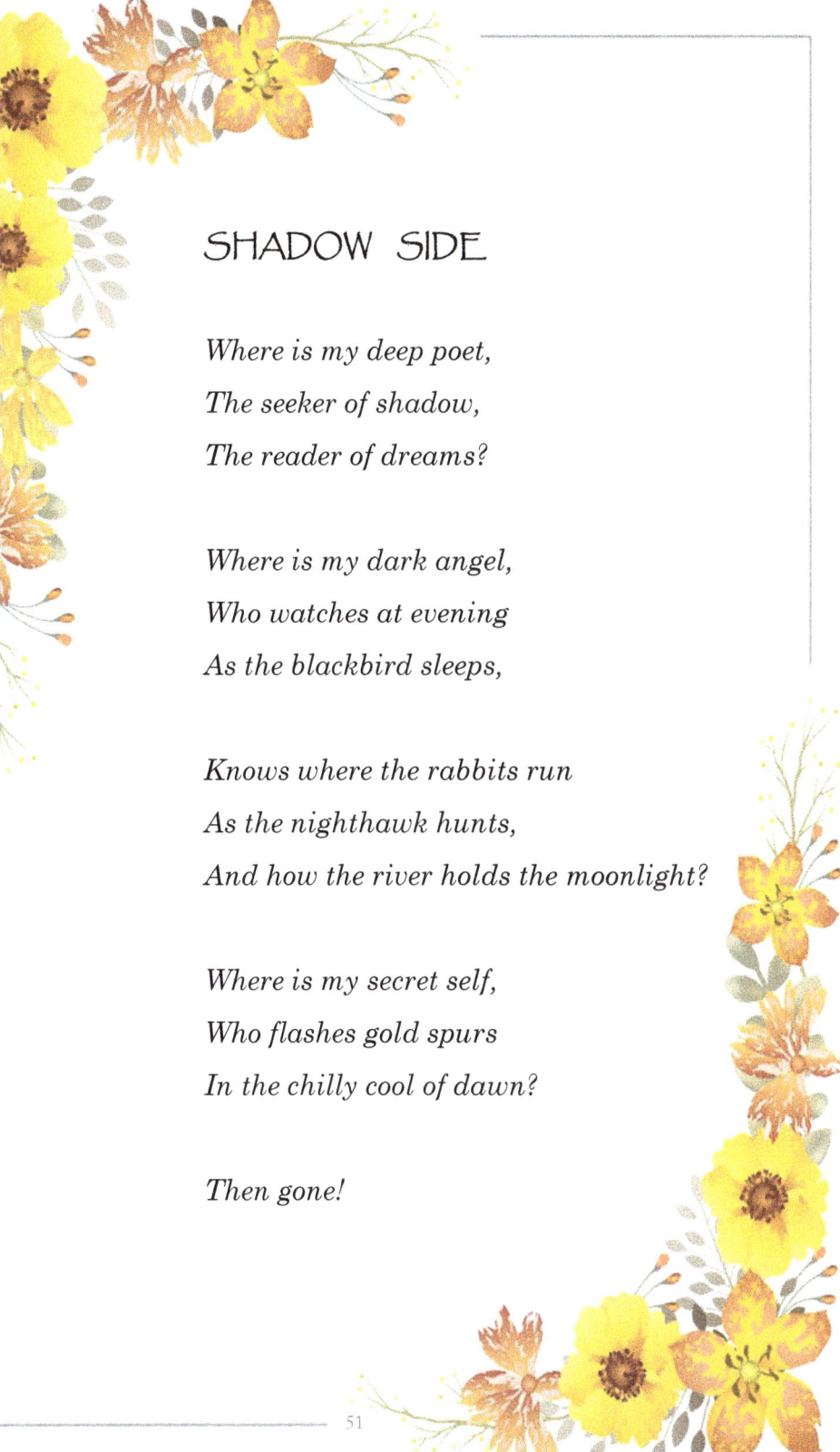

SHADOW SIDE

Where is my deep poet,
The seeker of shadow,
The reader of dreams?

Where is my dark angel,
Who watches at evening
As the blackbird sleeps,

Knows where the rabbits run
As the nighthawk hunts,
And how the river holds the moonlight?

Where is my secret self,
Who flashes gold spurs
In the chilly cool of dawn?

Then gone!

YIN / YANG

We are always
At the present moment,
The sum total
Of all our past decisions,
All our future dreams.

Ah, not so,
Says the stranger.
We are the sum total
Of that quiet being
Who lives in the presence
Of the ever-present now.

Both thoughts true.
As sister and brother,
A little bit of each
Is planted in the other.

A DRUNKEN DRAGONFLY

I am the deep black ink
That keeps the stars afloat.
I am the endless cosmic night.

I am the life force of every living thing.
I am your blood, your secret heart, your soul.
I am where your spirit goes at death.

I am the measure of wisdom and compassion,
And to whom all great religions call,
Though they've yet to speak My language well.

I write the music of the spheres
And teach the birds to sing it.
I am your prayers answered.

And still, you do not know Me.
Won't catch My name on solar winds,
Or hear My voice in ocean waves.

You're like a drunken dragonfly
That rips his wings off
While in the midst of flight.

WAKE UP!
You're missing quite a show.

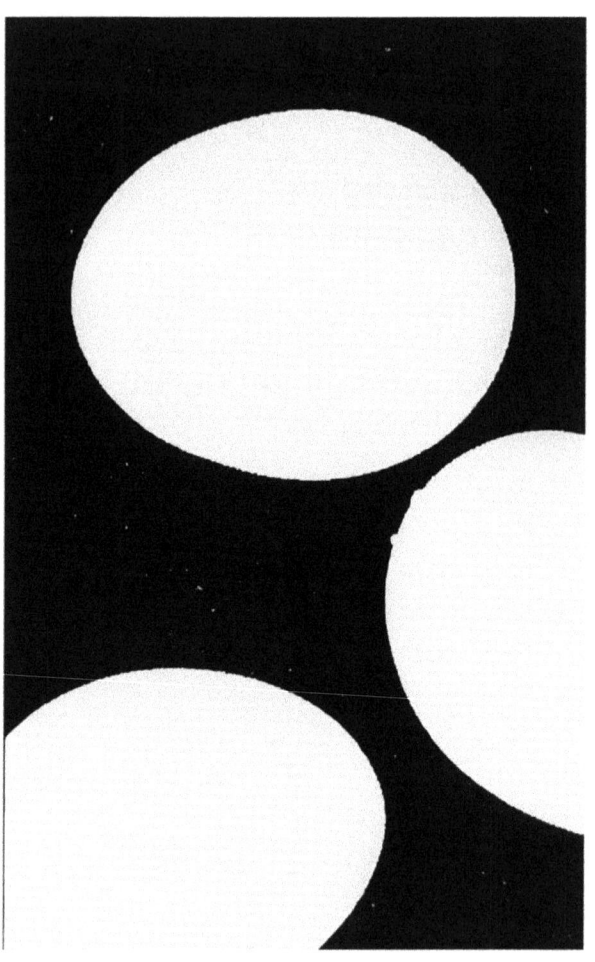

TO THE BLUE CRANE
AT GARLAND RANCH

Blue Crane

Sees me.

I see him.

Marsh reeds

Long stems

Find an artful way

For the Blue Crane

To blend with

An early fog-filled day.

Yet, the Blue Crane

Sees me

And I see him.

PRINCE W

The Prince rode in
With a golden lance.
He yearned for power,
He took his chance
  He stole the crown.

He suffered a wound
As he walked the hall
On the marbled floor
Of the castle tall.
  And so he bled.

All his knights sent out
With armor bright,
Along the borders,
Prepared to fight.
  And so they stood.

The land grew cold,
The crops grew dry.
Long shadows fell
Over earth and sky.
  The wide world changed.

Now, like Parsifal,
A young man comes
Up to the castle
And chants and drums,
  "What ails you, Prince,
  what ails you?"

THE HUMMINGBIRDS

To those who have never
Lived in Middle world,
That space somewhere
Between earth and heaven,

To all you strong and sturdy ones
Not crushed by an army of a
Thousand colored billboards,
A tangle of a million
New cemented freeways,
By each new
Trumped-up war.

I salute you!

But don't tread on us
So heavily.
Don't brush away
The feather-covered ones —
The Hummingbirds.

We have a certain strength,
Though it may be fading
With each new decade.
You will be losing much
By losing us.

TO RUN ALONE

I am too responsible of late,
Keeping needs and hopes behind a heavy gate,
Letting "Wondergirl" run wild about
Shutting pain and feelings out.

Once in a while my heart breaks through the ice
Of that cold, gray lake it's drowned in twice,
And stings me with its hot reality
That you and your love are not here with me.

I run alone so well, it just seems right
To give my all on this long and solo flight.
But since you've touched me with your face
It seems now a sad and sorry race —

To run alone.

LIVE WIRE FENCE

Had I only known one touch
Would send shots of lightning
Thru my bones and heart and skin
So sharp and deep, a bolt of raw electric

To scorch my body up and down
Singe my hair and upper lip
Burn holes in my socks and shoes
Searing thru the floor and into the cellar.

Had I only thought one touch
Could blind my eyes
So they could not see the present
Scorch my ears
So they could not hear the now
Leaving me stuck and staring at the past.

What once was tranquil
Is burnt to ashes by the heat.
Yet after all this carnage,
I want another touch.

THOUGHTS SOUTH

Leaving me alone
With your resounding silence
Overwhelms my thoughts.

Keeping still
And not moving toward me
Engages me entirely.

A slow rope burn
Drags across my chest
Deep toward my heart.

I'd rather fall to hell
And get it over with,
Than this.

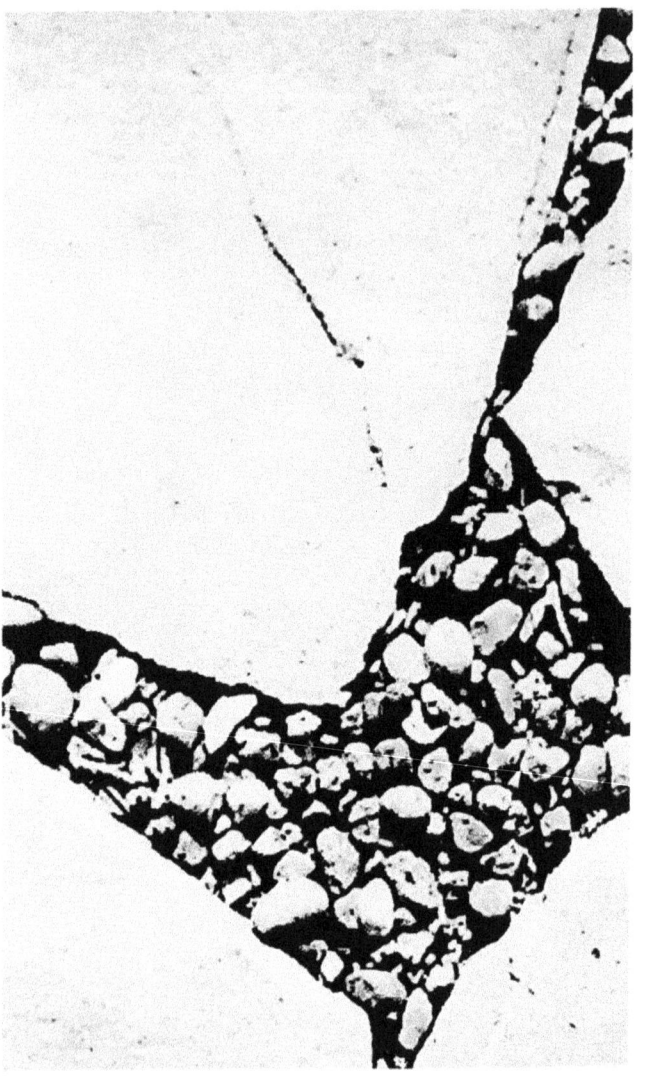

LA LOBA

I am a wolf
Wild, sleek and grey
I hunt by night
I sleep by day.

No one can catch me
No one's as swift.
From one hill to another
I silently shift.

You may see me at dawn
At daybreak's first light,
A flash of wildness,
I'm a dazzling sight.

There's dew on my coat
Mud on my paws
Blood on my mouth
And meat in my jaws.

I am a wolf
Wild, sleek and grey
I hunt by night
I sleep by day.

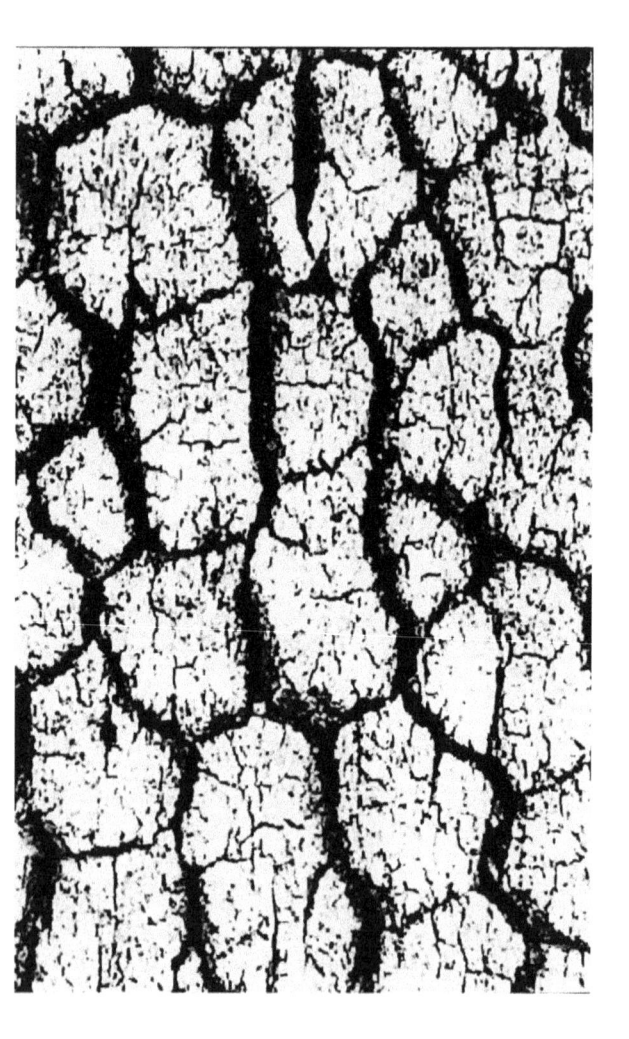

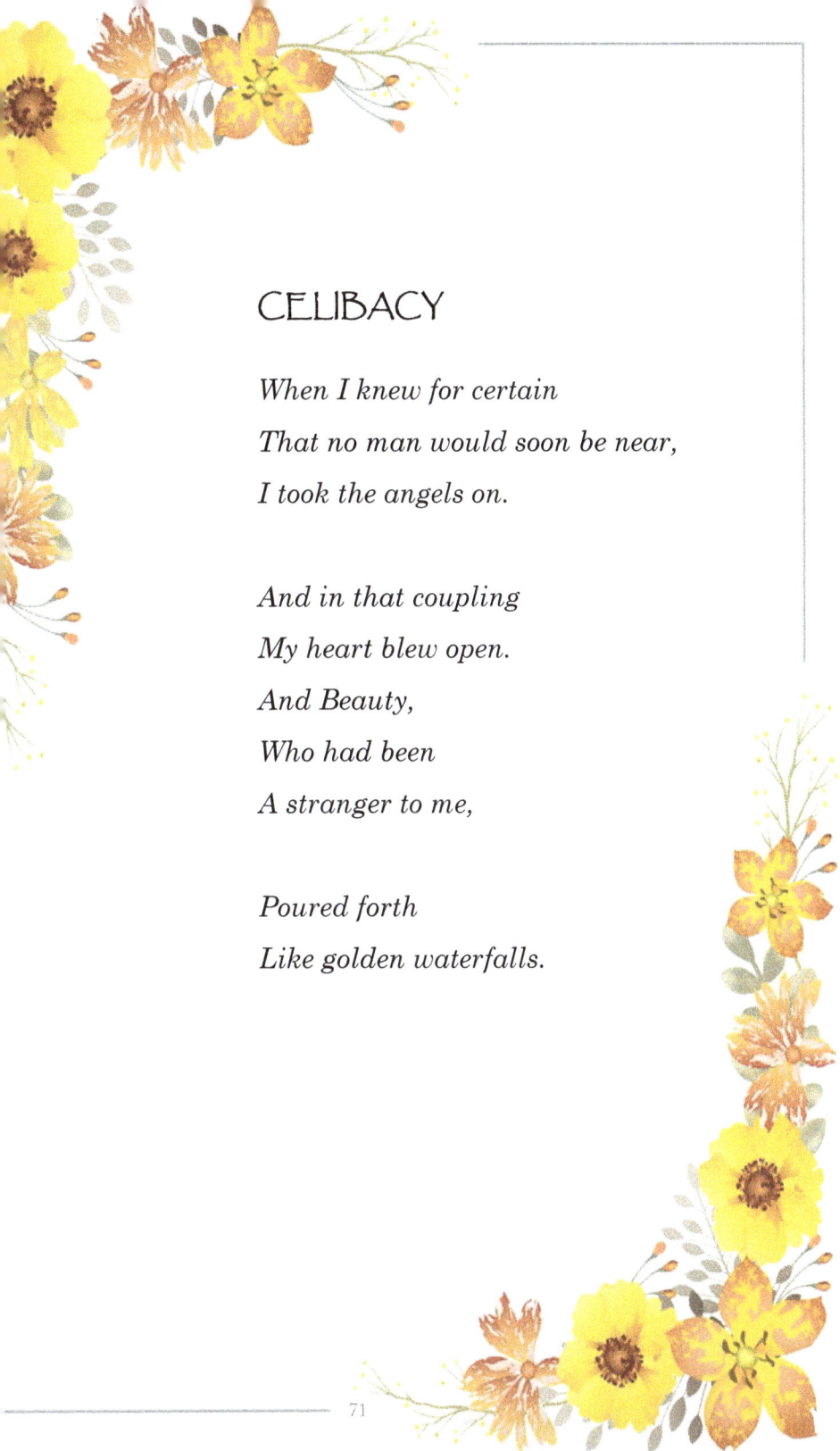

CELIBACY

When I knew for certain
That no man would soon be near,
I took the angels on.

And in that coupling
My heart blew open.
And Beauty,
Who had been
A stranger to me,

Poured forth
Like golden waterfalls.

GARLAND RANCH SUMMER

Heartbreakable star-drenched sky
Velvet black in deep July,
My blood turns to honey wine,
Warmed by the breath
Of ocean winds that drift
Through tall and flaxen wheat
On waves of summer heat.

Our skin turns pink, then peach, then tan
And sweet apricot juice stains
My shirt and hand,
While your hair is blown about
Like wild cornsilk in the breeze.

Sweet July and August
Run together, and soon
We feel as young as
Any yearling doe under the moon
Grazing on fallen
Plums at night.

All but forgotten
Cold February's chill
Month of brittle bones
And frozen dawns
Without the bright orange sun's good will.

Stay, oh warm July!
And linger long.
Too soon comes the gray
Of winter's crushing wheel,
When blood turns again to blood
And bones to steel.

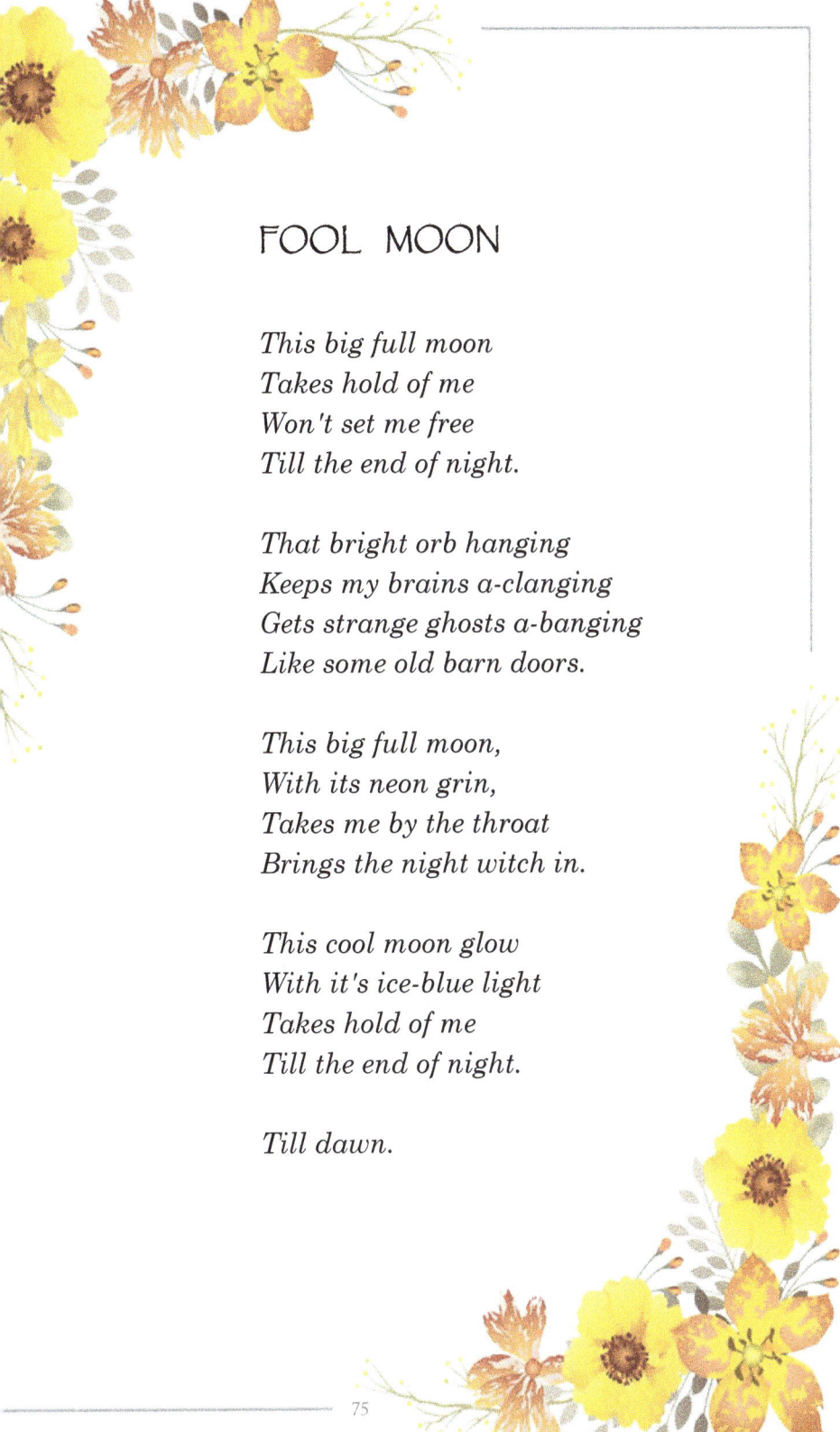

FOOL MOON

This big full moon
Takes hold of me
Won't set me free
Till the end of night.

That bright orb hanging
Keeps my brains a-clanging
Gets strange ghosts a-banging
Like some old barn doors.

This big full moon,
With its neon grin,
Takes me by the throat
Brings the night witch in.

This cool moon glow
With it's ice-blue light
Takes hold of me
Till the end of night.

Till dawn.

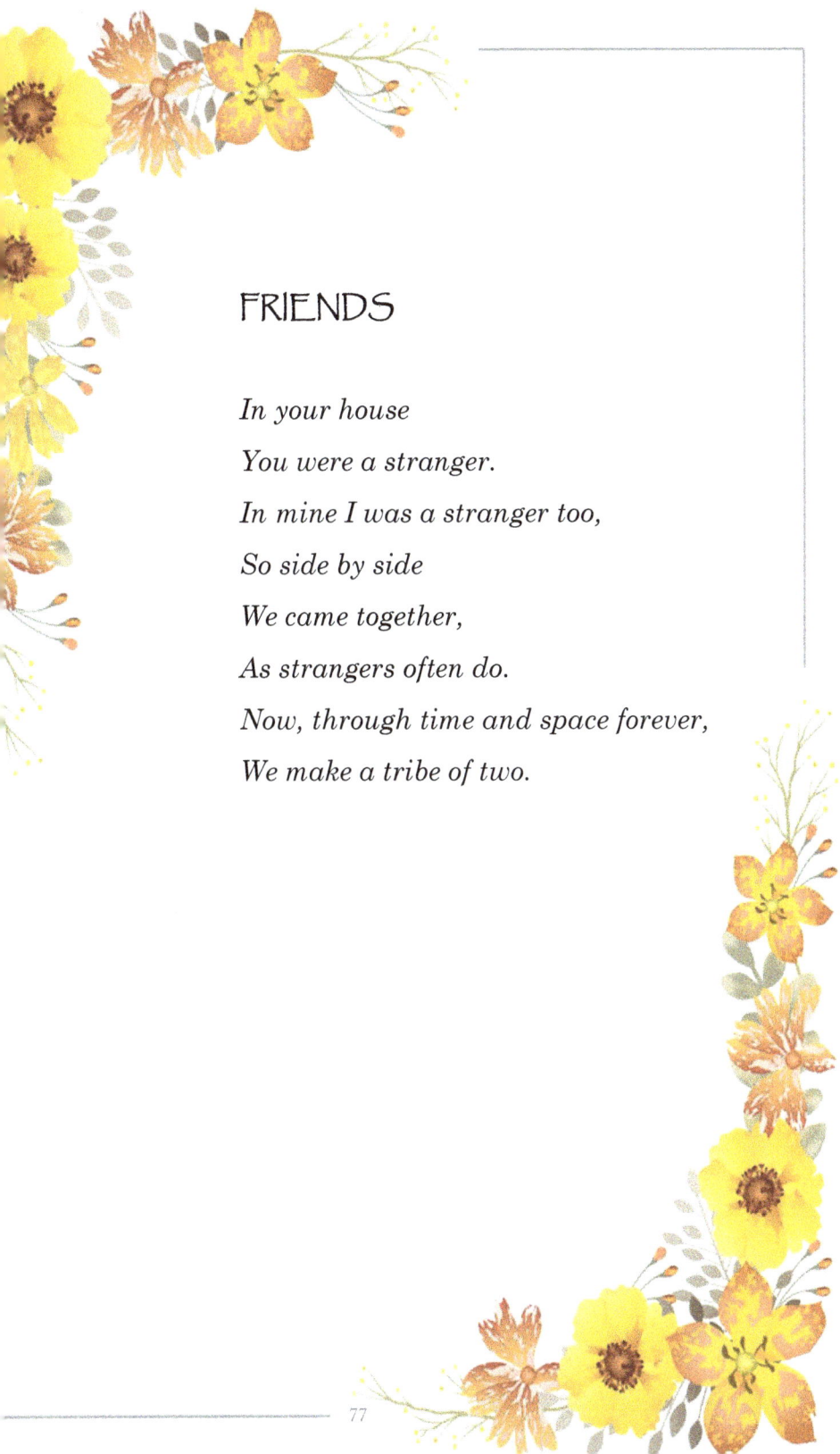

FRIENDS

In your house
You were a stranger.
In mine I was a stranger too,
So side by side
We came together,
As strangers often do.
Now, through time and space forever,
We make a tribe of two.

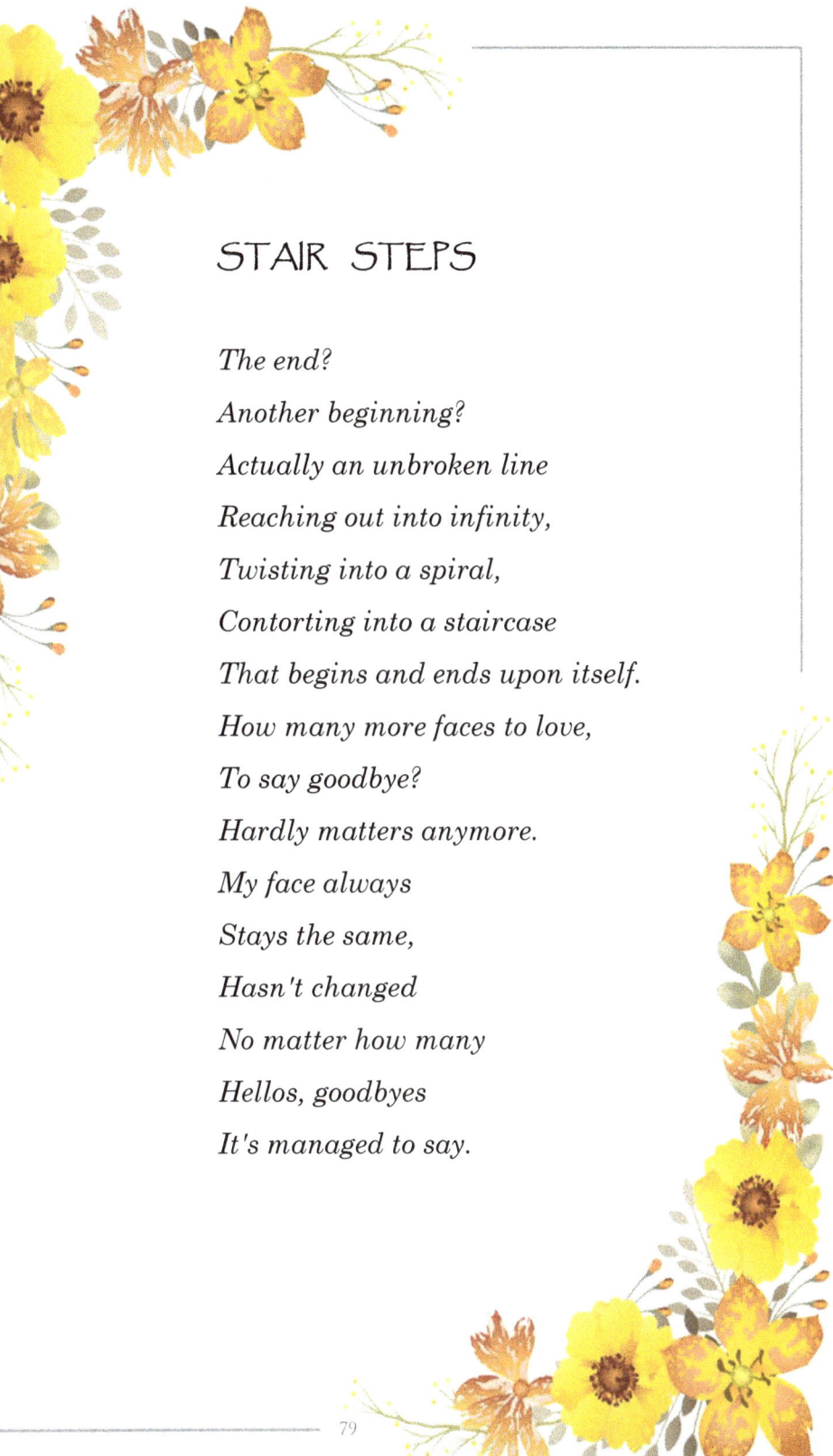

STAIR STEPS

The end?
Another beginning?
Actually an unbroken line
Reaching out into infinity,
Twisting into a spiral,
Contorting into a staircase
That begins and ends upon itself.
How many more faces to love,
To say goodbye?
Hardly matters anymore.
My face always
Stays the same,
Hasn't changed
No matter how many
Hellos, goodbyes
It's managed to say.

OCTOBER

Sweet October sings a haunting song
Of chilly days and frosted nights,
Yet she gaily goes along
In her resplendent robes
Of red and golden lights.

Summer's past her prime
Yet she still charms
With all the force
Of her adolescent way,
Along the meadows and the farms
Filled high with harvest
Where all the season's treasures lay.

While October
Hums an ancient tune
That tells of fear and dread,
Beneath her autumn sky
Of bright stars
And harvest moon,
She has a dagger hidden
In her glowing gown of red.

She shivers hard and long,
Causing cold bones
Dark nights to splinter.
She shudders with a chill so strong,
For she knows that all too soon,
She'll have to sleep
With Winter.

TWO THIEVES

Age steals youth away,
Death steals more.
Age dusts the windows,
Death shuts the door.

Age takes beauty,
Death, hope of spring.
Age takes laughter,
Death — everything.

Age steals thoughts away
And times once known
Age takes memories,
Death leaves its own.

Age knows good times
Death knows none.
Age takes many,
Death — everyone.

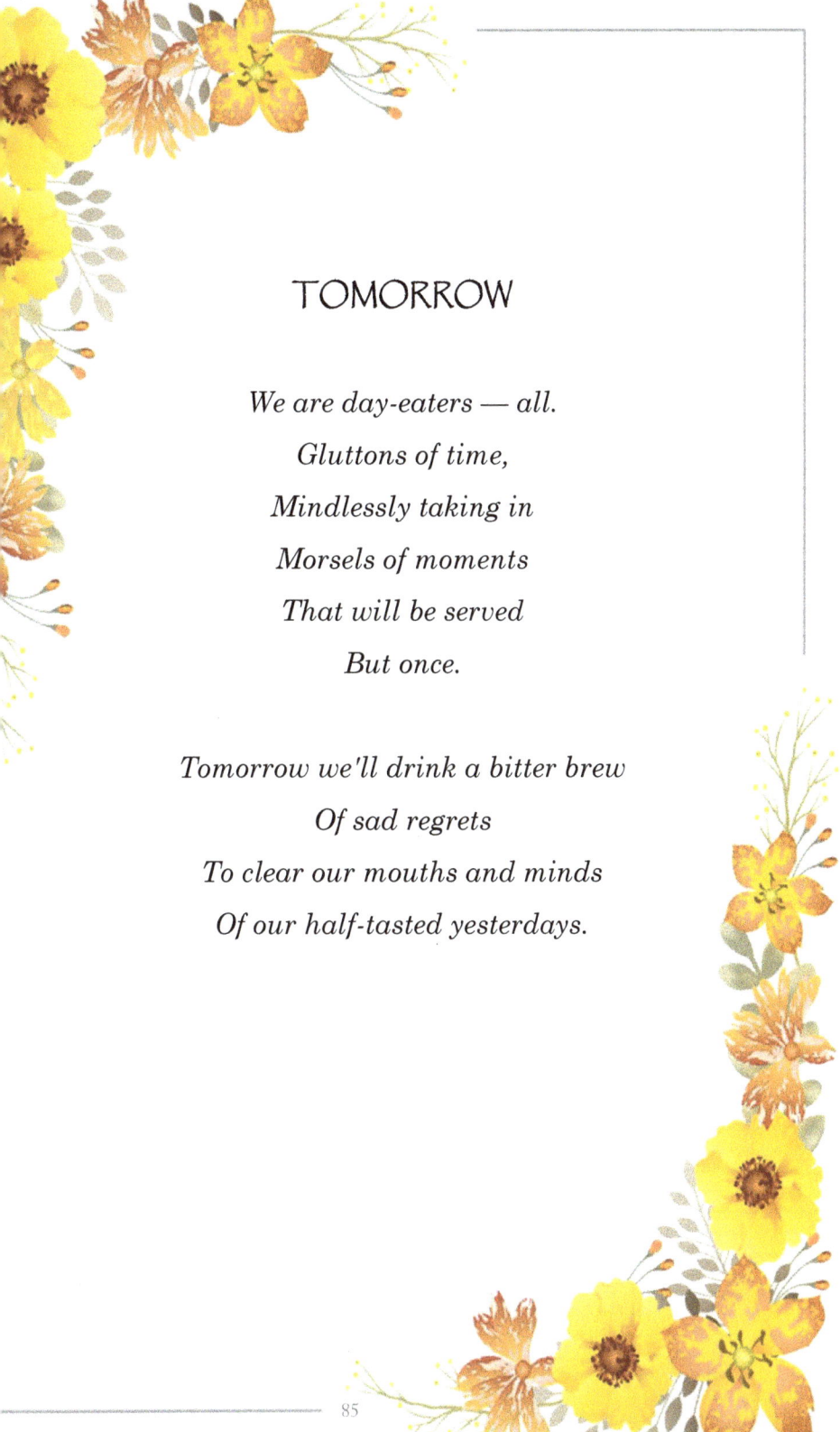

TOMORROW

We are day-eaters — all.
Gluttons of time,
Mindlessly taking in
Morsels of moments
That will be served
But once.

Tomorrow we'll drink a bitter brew
Of sad regrets
To clear our mouths and minds
Of our half-tasted yesterdays.

THE SCREAM

A sharp red sliver
Of a long high scream
Cuts the black silk night
To ribbons

With that, I knew
The night and the scream
Were mine,
Black silk ribbons,

And all.

TIME

Willowy aftermath
Of half-remembered dreams.

Gossamer mist dividing
Today from forever.

We watch our hours
From a door beyond,

And pass thru
In silken slippers.

EDUARDO

When you've finally tired
Of tasting all the silver fruit;
When you've caught
All the golden fish
The seas can hold,
Picked every summer flower,

When at last
The cup is emptied,
The searching done,
And you pause,
Remember one lone heart
That truly loved you.
Recall that one soul
Touched your fleeting soul
And shared the presence
Of a certain peace.

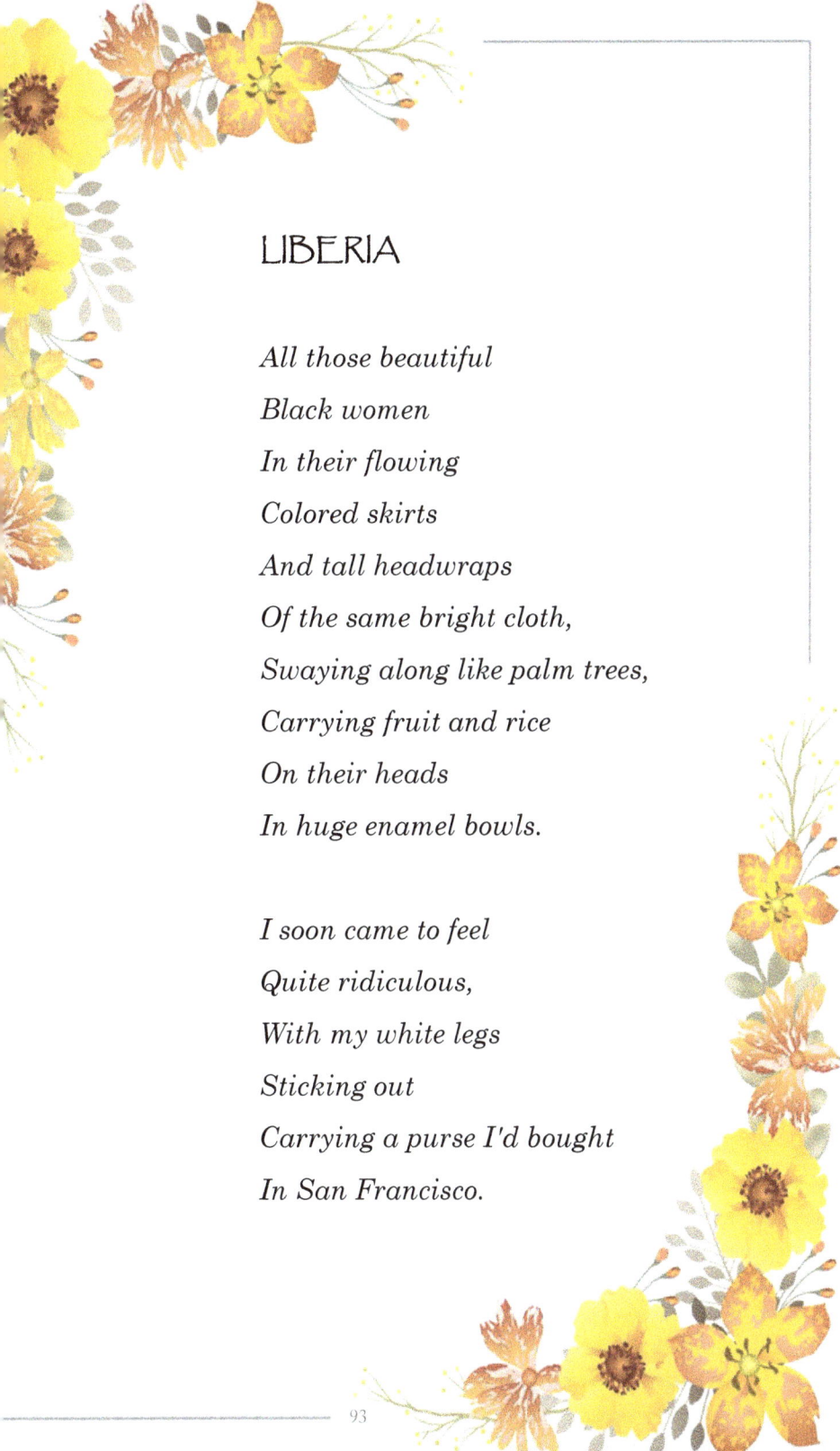

LIBERIA

All those beautiful
Black women
In their flowing
Colored skirts
And tall headwraps
Of the same bright cloth,
Swaying along like palm trees,
Carrying fruit and rice
On their heads
In huge enamel bowls.

I soon came to feel
Quite ridiculous,
With my white legs
Sticking out
Carrying a purse I'd bought
In San Francisco.

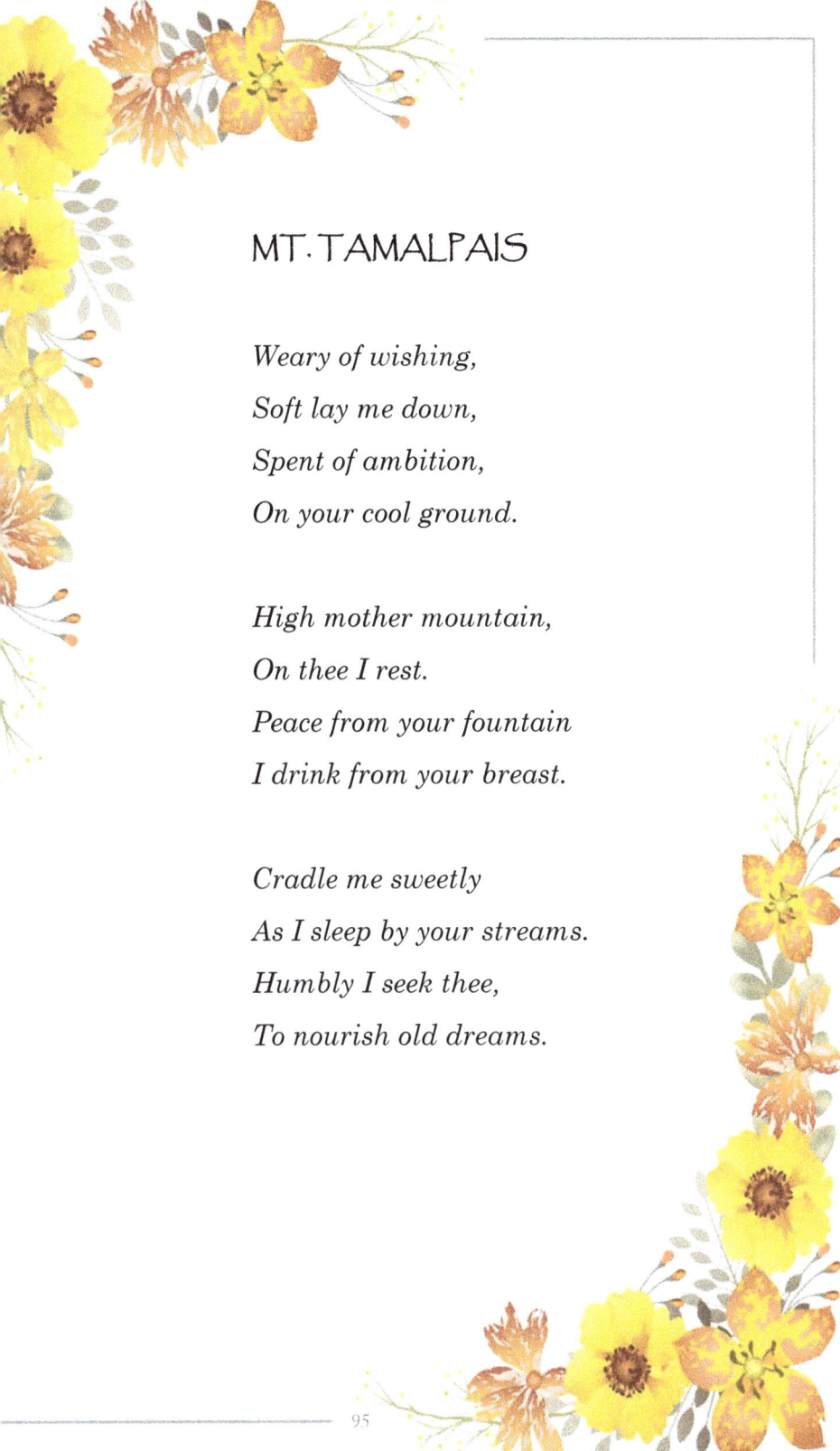

MT. TAMALPAIS

Weary of wishing,
Soft lay me down,
Spent of ambition,
On your cool ground.

High mother mountain,
On thee I rest.
Peace from your fountain
I drink from your breast.

Cradle me sweetly
As I sleep by your streams.
Humbly I seek thee,
To nourish old dreams.

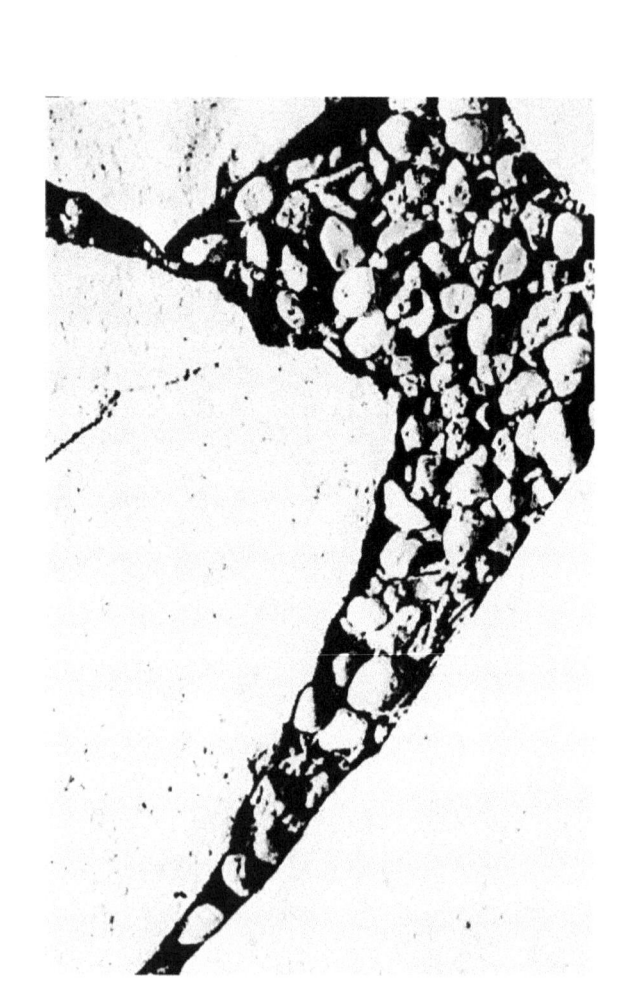

LOVE SONG

A flutter of emotion,
Then sudden flight
On frantic wings.

Freed,
From a twice-locked cage
My hopes when flying

To sing silent notes of need
Upon your windowsill.

CALIFORNIA GOODBYE

We've filled our basket with roses,
With bits of dark autumn moss:
Bright beads of dew from springtime
Last winter's delicate frost.

We fashioned coats of velvet
To wrap us from the wind,
Bought sweet wine from far off places,
Crystal glasses to pour it in.

We waded thru silken rivers
With fish carved of amethyst
Tied ribbons of rainbow around our waists
Wove threads of gold wheat for our wrists.

Though my heart is filled high with sorrow
I'm letting go of your hand
For I'm off to another beginning
Hoping you'll understand.

TO LAGUNITAS
AND BACK

Today was Memorial Day.
I wasn't invited to any picnics.
I did, however, have some fun.
Rode my bike up White's Hill
Hot, tired, face beating,
Flying down the other side
Calling out, "Sweet Jesus,"
All that cool wind in my hair.

I stopped and had a Pepsi
In front of a little store in Forest Knolls
To watch all the lovers
Off to picnics in wild Olema.

Back on the bike again,
Blowing down the hill again,
Rear end up,
Shoulders down,
Thinking —
Thank God for Memorial Day!

WILD HORSES

Where are all the wild hot stallions
That sped across my landscape?
With flashing hooves and blood-red eyes,
With steaming flesh and panting breath,
They tore through tender land,
Kicked up soul and sinew.

Let by one young white one,
Passion was his name,
Passion was his life,
And Freedom followed at his neck
Across my fresh green earth.
So wild and huge and free they ran,
With many more behind them.
Through white of day and blue of night,
Up hills of wonder, down valleys of regret.
They stopped for none, nor knew a master.

Now I only hear their echo,
Feel but the last of shaking earth.
They're all but gone,
Riding toward another golden sun,
Another promised land.
As I must stay,
To taste the dust of mine.

THE HOLY SPIRIT

I am the house of fire,
And on I'll burn
As I do now —
Forever blazing.

I'm not the owner
Of this flame,
I am but the space
For its existence.

Not blood
Flows through my veins,
But fire.
That fire alone can cool,
And yours alone.

I CHING DAYS

Time enough
For all things
You need to know.
Take time to savor
Every life lesson.

So quiet the many
Accept the multilevel.
No need for conflict,
Space abounds within.

The varied forces
Suspend themselves
In perfect alignment;
Simply allow them.

THE DANCER

A novelette of delicacy,
A living poem
Of contradictions,
Of dreams and coarse reality,
A sideshow of a sideshow,
Yet all the while
The main event.

Drinking the beer,
Singing the songs,
Laughing, breathing, living,
All, all with the eye of an artist
Splashes of oil paint
All over her dress.

The clown of a million sighs,
The leprechaun of a thousand words,
Knee-deep in life
Yet far above the curtained stage.

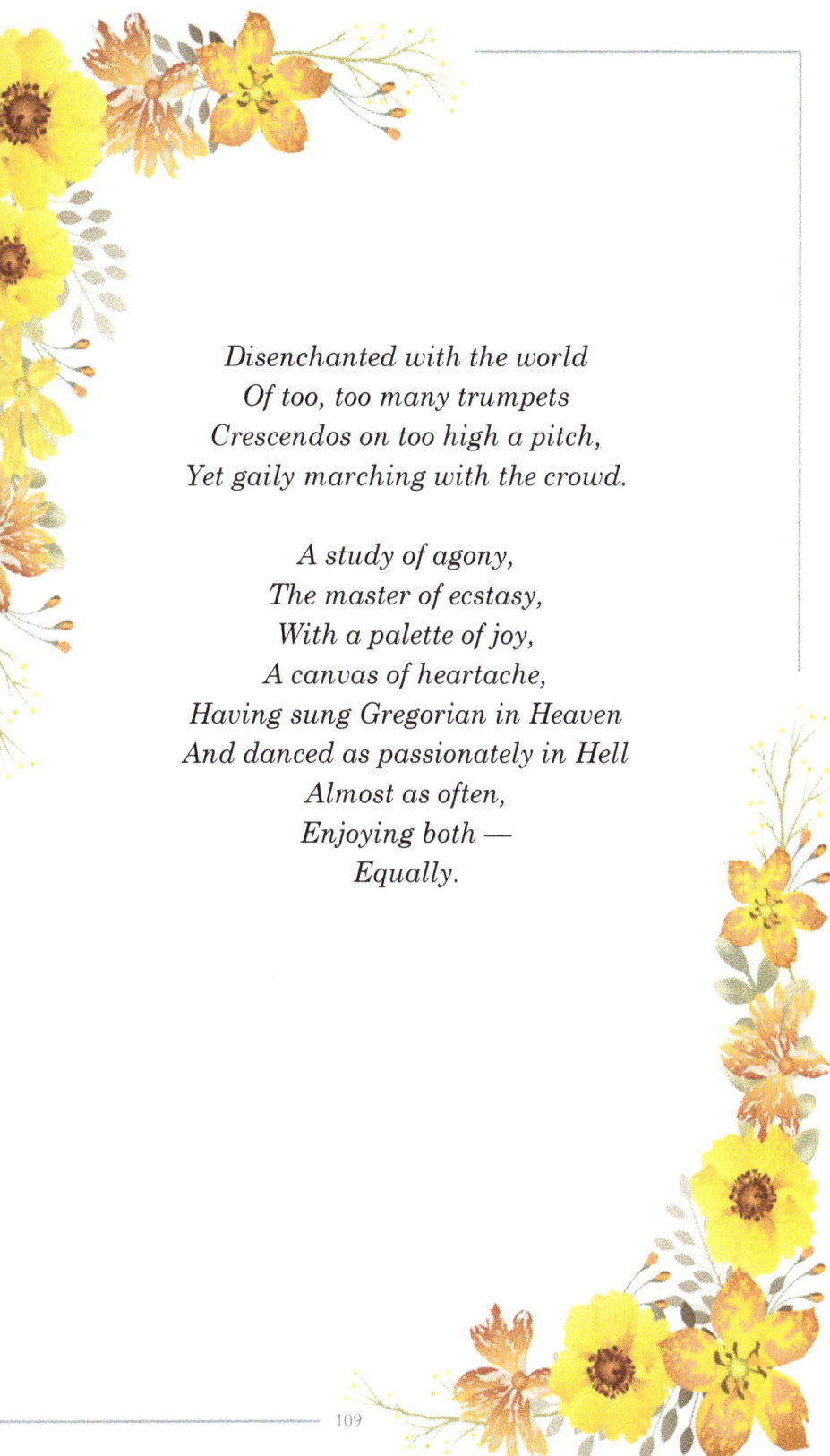

Disenchanted with the world
Of too, too many trumpets
Crescendos on too high a pitch,
Yet gaily marching with the crowd.

A study of agony,
The master of ecstasy,
With a palette of joy,
A canvas of heartache,
Having sung Gregorian in Heaven
And danced as passionately in Hell
Almost as often,
Enjoying both —
Equally.

NIGHT FLIGHT

My heart, where will you go tonight,
Where will the soft wind take you?
Where is the end of your lonely flight,
Back to the dreams that will break you?

Stay, my heart. This I implore.
Oh, must you go a-flying?
For, when you leave to muse once more,
Here must I stay a-dying.

Take thee, then, to the dreams so dead,
But when you return here tomorrow,
Expect me not a tear to shed,
When you come home — sick with sorrow.

ACKNOWLEDGEMENTS

I want to thank:

Todd Black for design and publishing,

Julie Cresswell for editing support,

Mary Badarak for technical support,

Michael Zeilik for technical support,

Mary Lausten for moral support; and,

Friends and neighbors of Cochiti Lake for support

of my first book.

www.ingramcontent.com/pod-product-compliance
Lightning Source LLC
Chambersburg PA
CBHW051215120626
46547CB00013B/1361